I dedicate this book to the therapists (yes, I mean plural) that have helped me deal with my anxiety. I have gotten counseling several different times in times of crisis in my life. Anxiety runs in my family. I actively manage my anxiety. I am so thankful to the therapists who have helped me over the years.

Does your child have a friend, family member, or classmate who has anxiety? Would you like your child or the children in your classroom to understand more about anxiety? Are you looking for an engaging way to start a dialogue about anxiety? I wrote this book to help solve these challenges.

A is for Anxiety is a children's picture book in an ABC format. With delightful illustrations, this book teaches typical feelings that many people with anxiety share. It also reviews some simple strategies to help manage anxiety. A child with anxiety narrates this book from his (or her) point of view. I intentionally left the character's gender up to the discretion of the reader.

A is for Anxiety provides an entertaining way to start a simple educational discussion about anxiety. I invite you to read this story interactively with your child. You can discuss the feelings this child has in this book. Encourage discussions of how you or people you love might be like the child in this book. You might compare and contrast how the child in this book is similar or different from a person you know with anxiety.

This book provides terrific opportunities to discuss how to be a friend of a child with anxiety. As a pediatric physical therapist, I work with children who have anxiety. Others often misunderstand the actions and behaviors of people with anxiety. I believe knowledge helps break down barriers and encourages kindness and patience. Assisting children to understand anxiety at a young age is powerful. Reading this book has the potential to change your child's perceptions of people with anxiety.

A is for Anxiety

Published by Gotcha Apps, LLC
1904 ½ Williams St.
Valdosta, GA 31602

Copyright © 2021 Amy E. Sturkey, PT

All rights reserved. No part of this publication may be reproduced, stored in a retrieval system or transmitted, in any form or by any means, electronic, mechanical, photocopying, recording, or otherwise, without prior written permission from the author.

This book provides general information on anxiety. It should not be relied upon as recommending or promoting any specific diagnosis or method of treatment. It is not intended as a substitute for medical advice or direct diagnosis and treatment of anxiety by a qualified physician or therapist. Readers who have questions about anxiety or its treatment should consult with a physician, counselor or other qualified health care professional.

ISBN: 978-0-9981567-9-8

Cover art and interior artwork by Ikos Ronzkie
Text by Amy E. Sturkey, PT

written by
Amy E. Sturkey, PT

illustrated by
Ikos Ronzkie

A is for Anxiety.

Anxiety is different from fear. Fear is your body's built-in alarm system that protects you from real danger. You feel fear when you see a shark while swimming. You are afraid when you hear a car beep when you are crossing the street. Anxiety is worrying about the future. Anxiety can be about real situations, but they aren't happening right now. It feels like fear, but the danger might or might not be real. The situation might not even happen. I worry about what could go wrong too much, too easily, and way too long.

B is for the Bottom of my stomach.
For me, that is where anxiety starts.
My stomach feels like it is tied in a knot.
My heart pounds. My head hurts.
I shake and sweat. I breathe fast.
My whole body tightens up.
I get nightmares, and I can't sleep.

C is for Catastrophe.

That is when I think that everything that can go wrong will go wrong, that no one will be there to help me, and that I am not strong enough to make it through by myself.

I see everything that happens as a sign that the worst is coming. I can't pay attention to anything else. I believe that I can't do anything right. I think I will fail. I am sure that I am stupid.

D is for Dangerous thinking.
That's when I can only focus on the worst possible endings. Then I get so scared that I can't think clearly. I become afraid about getting this afraid again. I wonder what others will think of me. I am so embarrassed. Why do I scream and cry so easily?

E is for Escape.
My anxiety gets so strong that I wish I could crawl in that hole and disappear! Maybe if I never go around the scary things, I won't be scared again? I try to warn everyone else to watch out too! Please tell me again and again that everything is going to be okay.

F is for my Feelings.
My out-of-control thinking makes me feel incredibly nervous. Different people have different anxieties. What thoughts make me feel anxious? I get so worried my parents won't come to get me. Bugs, dogs, doctors, and crowds all make me nervous. I constantly worry about making mistakes and not being perfect.

I can't stop thinking about how people might laugh at me. I can get so worried that I can't eat, I can't sleep, I can hardly move.

G is for my Growing anxiety. The more I stayed away from all my worries, the more they scared me. The more I ran, the bigger and scarier my anxieties became. My parents tried to protect me, and then everything got worse! I never wanted to take a chance of facing my anxieties. I thought I couldn't fail if I never did anything. So, I wanted to stay home all the time.

H is for Help.
I realized avoiding the things that make me anxious wasn't working. My anxieties had grown too big to handle on my own, so I started counseling. The therapist helped me learn how to tame my anxieties. Counseling is a safe place to talk about my feelings and learn ways to deal with them.

I is for my Imagination.
My thoughts are powerful. I can imagine myself facing my anxieties and staying calm and strong. I can imagine my worry and change a part of it to look less scary or even funny. My counselor and parents help guide me in changing my thoughts from anxiety to power.

J is for Just breathe.
When I feel anxious, I put my hands on my belly and take a four-second deep breath in through my nose. Then I breathe out through my mouth for four seconds.

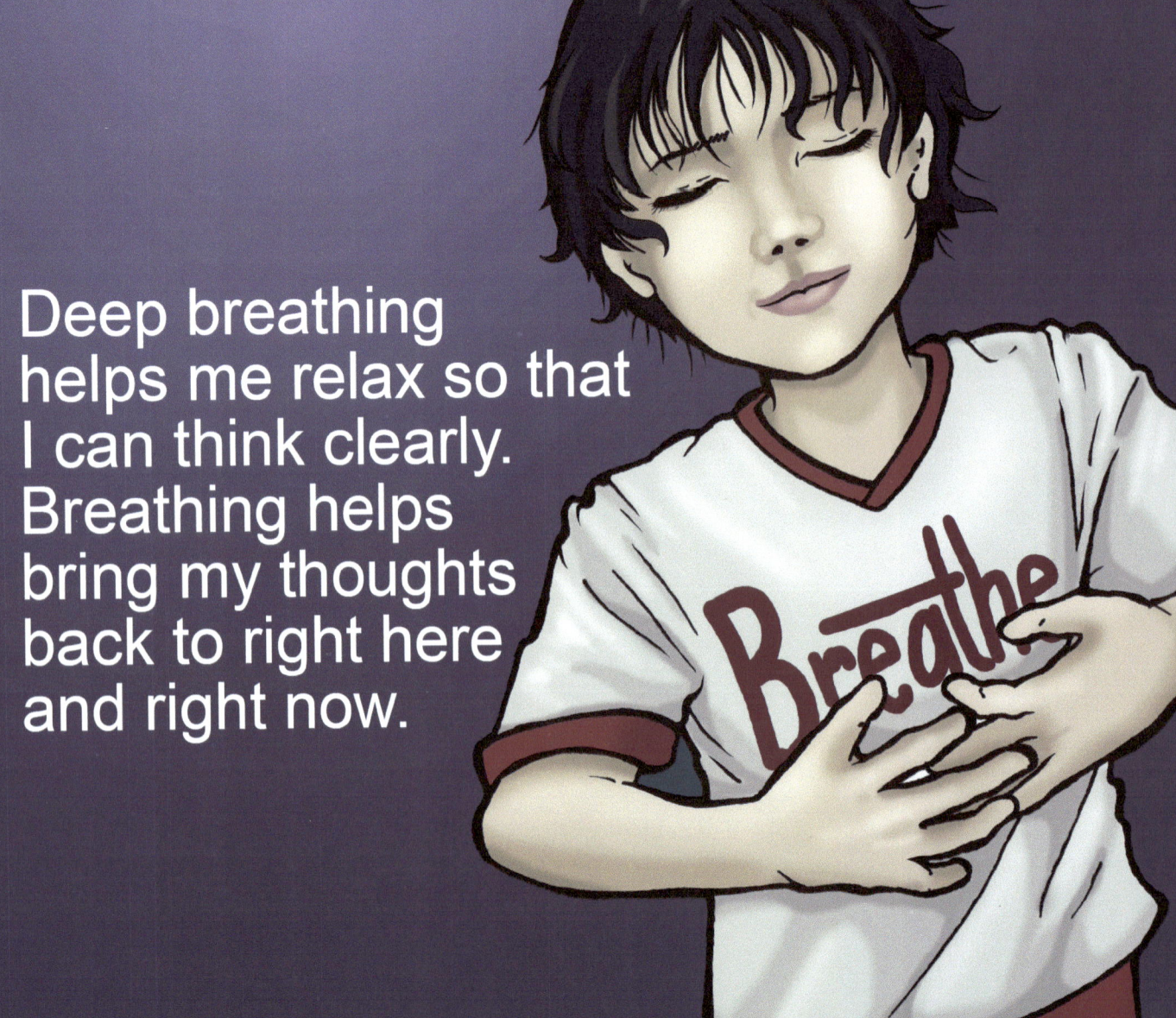

Deep breathing helps me relax so that I can think clearly. Breathing helps bring my thoughts back to right here and right now.

K is for Keeping taking baby steps. I don't have to tackle my anxieties all at once. My worry gets smaller and smaller each time I face my anxieties. I can take one step at a time.

L is for Losing my anxious thinking. These are the steps I took purposely to conquer my anxieties about making mistakes. I started by just imagining my mother making a mistake and being okay with it. Then I imagined myself making the same mistake and not getting upset! Then I learned a new dance step with my family. We all had trouble and laughed. Then I played a game with my best friend that was tricky. Later I played it with all the kids on my street. These small steps took me a few months but really helped me.

M is for Make a "control" list.

I make lists of what I can completely control, what I can sort of control, and what I can't control at all. Then I can see where I can take control. For example, I am afraid of bugs. I can completely control the bug spray I use and the clothes I wear. I have some control over what time I go outside and the thoughts I have about bugs. However, I have no control over the bugs which might visit me when I am outdoors. So I work to change the things I have control over.

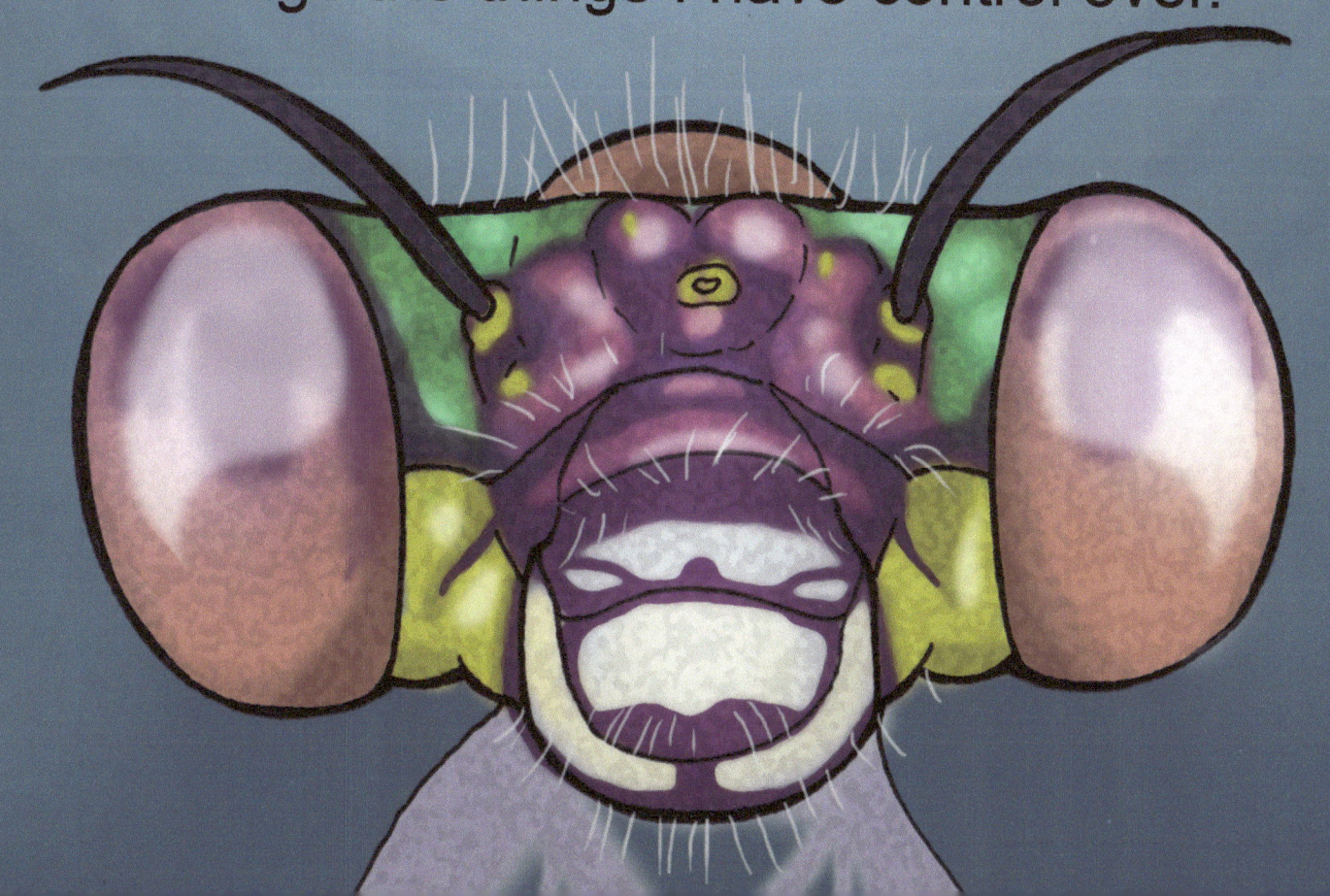

N is for Need.
I've learned that I need to talk about my feelings. Sometimes I draw my feelings with paint, markers, or finger paint. I give my emotions a color and a shape. The more I understand my feelings, the more I have control over them.

O is for Okay.
I remind myself when I get anxious about crowds that I will be okay. I learned self-talk. I can tell myself helpful thoughts that are kind and calming. I tell myself things like, "I am okay right now. I am safe right now." I focus on the present instead of worrying about the future.

P is for Parents.
Mom said when she was my age, she had some of the same anxieties. She wishes she had a team to help her work through her anxiety. Now she talks to me about how she feels and what her plan is when she feels anxious. Watching her helps me.

Q is for Quieting my mind.
When I feel anxious, my thoughts run around like a race car going around the same track. I am learning to meditate, relax, and focus my mind on the present. As I control my thoughts and quiet my mind, I control my anxiety.

R is for keeping it Real.
Dad says life is not usually perfect, but it usually isn't the worst possible either. Usually, life is somewhere in the middle. Is it possible a dog will bite me? Yes. Is it likely a dog will bite me? No. Dad says you are never 100% safe, but you can't stop living and enjoying life.

S is for celebrating "Sometimes." I used to think terrible things happened "every" time. I felt good things "never" happened. I was confused and thought my anxiety would be "forever." Now I see that "sometimes" is a great word too. "Sometimes" I might be anxious, but "sometimes" I might not be. I am getting more confident. My family, friends, and therapist will help when "sometimes" things don't go so well.

T is for Thinking Things Through.
Okay, what if the worst happens? What happens if Dad is late picking me up from school. What could I do? I could talk to the teacher. She could call my parents. Someone would stay with me until Mom or Dad came to pick me up. Talking through what would happen helps me put my worrying to rest.

U is for Understanding that anxiety can take time to change. My therapist helps my family and me as I get braver. Sometimes medication is necessary, sometimes not. I must learn to be patient and trust my parents and therapist. I am getting stronger and less scared.

V is for Victory.

Now I understand when I hide from my anxiety, my anxiety wins and grows stronger. When I face my anxiety, I win, and I grow stronger. I can't run away and beat this. But, I can decide who gets the victory. With the help from my family and counselor, I know I can be the winner.

W is for Work.

Learning to control my anxiety is hard work. I have to practice. My parents thank me for how hard I try when I am anxious. I know that sometimes I won't be as successful, but thank you for supporting me as I learn to be more confident and brave.

X is for the all-important eXtras. Taking care of your mind means taking care of your body too. When dealing with anxiety, eating healthy foods, exercising sixty minutes a day, and getting plenty of sleep are super important. They give me the energy I need to fight my anxiety.

Y is for Yay!
I am super excited you know about anxiety now. Having friends understand how I feel makes me feel safe and supported.

Z is for Zap.
I wish I could Zap these worries with a blaster right out of here. But, with help from my family, therapist, and friends, I am on a path to mastering my anxieties. Now that you know more about anxiety, we can encourage each other when life gets tricky.

The End.

Common Themes for Anxiety by Age of the Child

Birth - 2 years: Separation from parents, strangers, loud sounds

2-3 years of age: Storms, the dark, animals, fire, and water

4-5 years of age: Insects, death, getting lost

5-7 years of age: Sickness, natural disasters, school

12-18 years of age: Performance anxiety, rejection by others

Other offerings by the author:

A is for Autism: A Child's View
D is for Down Syndrome: A Child's View
C is For Cerebral Palsy: A Child's View
A is for ADHD: A Child's View
Pediatric Physical Therapy Strengthening Exercises for the Hips
Pediatric Physical Therapy Strengthening Exercises for the Knees
Pediatric Physical Therapy Strengthening Exercises for the Ankles

Blog:
www.pediatricPTexercises.com

YouTube Channel:
Pediatric Physical Therapy Exercises

Facebook page:
Pediatric Physical Therapy Exercises

Instagram page:
Pediatric PT Exercises

Pinterest page:
amysturkey/pediatric-physical-therapy

Ikos Ronzkie

is an international graphic designer, book illustrator, and comic strip artist. She creates fanciful illustrations for advertisements, campaigns, comic books, character designs, book designs, and book covers. She has worked as an illustrator with local and international clientele for over 17 years.

She illustrated this author's previous books, *A is for Autism, D is for Down Syndrome, C is for Cerebral Palsy* and *A is for Attention Deficit Hyperactivity Disorder*. She is also the illustrator for books, including: *Pirate Sam, What's Wrong with Grandma?, Bamadiva books, Kutzow Town, Your Daily Happiness Boost, A Moving Tale, What Does Alex See, A Tea for Queen Bee* and *Willie Nillie Adventure* books.

Her clients include international publishers, dollmakers, comic book writers, authors, and picture book writers. She produces "Bayan ng Biyahero Comics" for the Antipolo Star Newspaper for the Rizal and Metro Manila distribution areas and produces weekly Comics in Free Fiction House. She previously created "Estudyante Blues" for the Living News and Good Education magazine. Independently, she writes and produces her own comics: "Karit," "Dalawang Liham," "Sulsi" and webcomics "Hilda Intrimitida and friends".

Ronzkie is the co-founder of IKOS Komiks and Allawig Studio, which strives to promote and explore Philippine culture with visual and literary arts. Their creations are dedicated to work inspired by the Philippine history, myths, and legends. She is also the publisher of an online newspaper, The Rizal Newsweek and the founder of Rusnest and Tropang Nanay.

www.ingramcontent.com/pod-product-compliance
Lightning Source LLC
Chambersburg PA
CBHW040019050426
42452CB00002B/49